Dedication

This book is dedicated to all those many [...]
their children would be able to see them [...]
but ultimately vain efforts the technique [...]
would not have been needed. If they had [...]
frustration and alienation may never have [...]
Courts to become the most exploited an [...]
system that it is today.

Author's Acknowledgements

The authors would like to thank:

- Our exs for bringing these strategies to our attention

- Our mothers for explaining them to us

- Our children for continuing to believe in us

- Numerous Judges, Solicitors and other Professionals for their apathy and disingenuousness

Contents

Preface

This book provides a wealth of sound advice on how to eliminate an unwanted parent from your life while retaining all the financial benefits. The tips and tricks in this book are tried and tested and have helped countless parents go from complicated and confusing sharing parenting arrangements to sole parenting of their children and a simpler, quieter life. It has also helped achieve the magnificent figure of 70% of children having no relationship with their non-resident parent after separation, which keeps this great nation of ours at the head of international league tables.

Never before has so much invaluable advice been brought together in one handy volume. No need to go hiring expensive solicitors or trawling through Gingerbread or Mumsnet, Parentectomy for Mummies covers all eventualities in easy steps, written in plain English. This book will help you simplify your life, extract the most from your ex-partner and your child's ex-parent; with additional chapters on grandparents, pension pots, extracting revenge and much more.

Any parent can do this and successfully get rid of the other parent. It doesn't need any special skills. Just harness the righteousness that lies dormant within all of us, and you will soon see the results. With the right approach you can continue to extract revenge for many years while ensuring you ex lives in penury and your children learn who to blame for just about everything.

While Family Court Judges have been vilified for years by fathers for pandering to mothers wishes, for massive gender bias and particularly for conspicuously failing to enforce their own Contact Orders; the writing of this volume has made the authors realise some of the difficulties the judges face from the sheer inventiveness of human nature. However, we cannot help but be filled with admiration and praise for their cowardice and lack of leadership in failing to stand up for gender equality or the interests of children, so that we can all sigh with relief and carry on following the same old exhausted case law that keeps children and fathers broken-hearted. How much bother this saves us! And how great is the gratitude of those mothers who are, of course, incapable of malice and are only concerned with the welfare of their children.

Introduction

We all know that feeling. The other parent has done their job by contributing some genetic material (inferior though that may be). You have three children under five round your feet all day and you don't need the fourth man-child who appears every evening claiming he has had a hard day at work and grumbles when you inform him politely you've been looking after his children all day and now it's his turn and you've got some very important soap opera time to catch up on.

Look no further. This little book will tell you how to eradicate this annoyance from your and the children's lives whilst still retaining your family's home and plenty of financial support to allow you to be a full time mother and concentrate on the children.

While those already involved in the Family Court system will be joyously familiar with what is written here, there will be many outsiders, such as those who are either happily married or have achieved a sensible and reasonable separation in their eyes and the eyes of their children and all those with no knowledge of the postcode/judicial lottery of the family courts who will say: 'This is impossible! People and courts simply could not be that biased, bitter, unfair or unreasonable!' Fear not! They really are! And it's so easy to exploit them!

Some commentators may say that there is no law in Family Law. It would be an exaggeration to say "no law", there is some, if you look hard. Those who frequent the Family Courts will know that most of the decisions rest on the discretion of the extremely wise and knowledgeable Family Judge (and on which side of the bed they got out of that day). So if your Judge can't think of a relevant section of the law, you really don't have to worry. They can make up as much as they need to fill the gap. Remember these are courts of law, not justice, you'll be absolutely alright even when you are completely in the wrong and only being malicious and vengeful, which you never are, of course.

Children and Families Act 2014 - Update

The new Children and Families Act came into force on 22nd April and introduces a range of measure which are intended to improve the operation of the Family Courts and encourage parents who are separating to resolve their issues out of court. Initially the draft of this bill included a presumption of shared parenting, which obviously would have been a complete disaster and devastated the Family Law Industry.

Fortunately various pressure groups and interested parties have managed to water down the provisions in this act so that it leaves decisions about parenting arrangements to the discretion of judges once again.

Some of the positive aspects are that parents will be forced to go to mediation prior to making a court application. If the right approach is employed, this can be used to delay any relationship with the redundant parent and place further financial burden on him with no tangible result. Hopefully he'll run out of money even sooner.

In addition there is now a 26 week time limit on the duration of cases, but this only applies to Public Law cases. Private Law cases can still take as long as you can string it out for, with no penalties.

Although the courts are not required to consider that any involvement by a parent in a child's life is beneficial, the concept of any division of time for the child between the parents is specifically excluded, so indirect contact is still an option for the courts. This is where the redundant parent writes birthday/Christmas cards and sends presents you can dispose of before your child gets upset by thinking their useless parent wants to see them or allows them to be fooled that he might be nice.

Chapter 1: What Every Aspiring Single Parent Should Know

For many years the fact of being a sole parent carried a stigma which persuaded some people to try and make a relationship work long after the feelings they once had for their other half had faded. People used to stay together (misguidedly) 'for the sake of the children'. Now thanks to largely female led academic research and the support of the Government and Family Courts, parents stuck in a dead end relationship can eliminate the annoying other parent from their own and their children's lives while retaining all the benefits. Being a single parent is now a source of pride and dignity.

This great revolution has come about through the dedicated work and lobbying of many committed individuals and organisations, too many to name here. Thanks to them you will have the arguments and confidence to explain why you got rid of a parent who seemed to all the world to be perfectly respectable, capable and caring. It may not have been obvious on the face of it, but it's explained in this book how you and your children have suffered years of abuse at the hands of that perpetrator, interfering with your parenting, confusing and distressing the children and making them love him, so that he can continue the abuse. There is so much support for single parents that you will be better off on your own with the children.

Nor do you have to worry that parenting will be too much of a burden. You can send the children to school, there's television and electronic games, and if you want to have a bit of "me time" there are childminders, after-school and holiday clubs to occupy the children while you're busy.

The best strategy is to have enough children while he's still with you to ensure your lifestyle won't have to change once he's gone. A local solicitor will advise you how many this is in your case, but it's generally one less than the number of bedrooms in your house, the extra bedroom being reserved for yourself.

Explain that he is violent towards you and that you are terrified of him while crying and shaking will convince any judge to grant you an ex-parte occupation and non molestation order on the spot.

You won't even have to tell him he has to leave, just get your Occupation Order, vacate the house, with the children for an hour or two at a given time and the police will come and turf him out, and ensure that he can't ever come back.

You have a natural right to retain all the family possessions, unless he gets a court order to the contrary. You can send him anything you don't want in a publicly embarrassing way such as putting his enormous, gas barbecue, chef's hat and apron, in a wheelbarrow and getting a relative to wheel it through the town to give back to him.

Make sure you destroy or sell any of his childhood possessions he has carefully kept to pass on to his children such as his Scalextric and other toys.

You should be charitable when he asks to have some of the possessions that you own. If you don't need it, you can arrange a time for him to come and collect these possessions. Make sure you and the children are out when he arrives, because you don't want them to see his wretched face and feel sorry for him. They may behave inappropriately, such as running and throwing their arms around him and crying out 'Daddy! Daddy!'.

While the children are at school and he's normally at work would be best. Bear in mind that he's never happy, so if he complains that a vital piece is missing, such as the remote control from the small television you let him have, make sure he knows you don't have it and that he must have lost it. He lost you, or you told him to get lost, so he can lose pretty much anything and must be getting used to it.

Get Professional Help From "The Experts"

They will gladly help in stopping your ex seeing the children. Professionals who may get involved are Cafcass Officer, Social Worker, Guardian, Psychologist, Paediatrician, GP, School, Children's Centre, Health Visitor. etc. etc. Involve as many as you can.

Explain how upset the children are at the thought of having to see their father. How they have sleepless nights and nightmares. How they beg you not to make them go. Tell these professionals you don't feel the children should be made to go to contact against their wishes. Tell them it's making you ill, get your doctor to diagnose you with depression and prescribe therapy. Tell them the whole court process is just making you ill. You ex keeps dragging you back to court and you will have a total collapse if it goes on. With any luck one or more of them will tell the court they think direct contact should be stopped because the detrimental effect on the mother is bad for the children. A wonderfully wise judge really did make this ruling, and everybody has followed it ever since.

Repeat the above information in every statement you make to the court. Ask for a psychological assessment of your ex as you feel there must be something wrong with him. This will waste at least 3 months or more and cost him a packet and with any luck they may find that he has a problem. Beware though, you will probably have to be assessed as well and the costs may have to be shared.

Ask that a Guardian ad Litem be appointed for the children to ascertain their feelings. This may take a little longer, but it's important to do things right. The extra time they have away from that awful man will allow you to help them understand how dangerous he is so they can express this to the Guardian and could result in a recommendation to the court for no contact. It will also add a third party to the court proceedings and your legal team plus the children's legal team will most probably be able to convince the judge that the children's father should be ignored.

Always have your solicitor send menacing letters to your ex on the Friday he picks up the children for contact. A very good time is the Friday before Christmas as your solicitor's office will then be closed for two weeks. . A good wheeze at this time is to have your solicitor send notice of a court action to demand financial support that is greater than your ex's income.

Chapter 2: All About Babies

You should be well rid of your ex by the time the last child is born. Since he's not going to be part of your child's life, it's best not to allow him at the birth. Unfortunately the Government has made the mistake of allowing fathers of children some rights to information about them. You can avoid this legal technicality by ensuring all the child care professionals (Teachers, GPs, Social Services etc.) are informed by you that they are not to allow the father access to information, school reports, attendance at school events etc. You will be amazed and delighted to find that they are blithely ignorant of the law, and automatically comply with your wishes.

It is often inconvenient to have him on the Birth Certificate as it may impact on the benefits you can receive from the State. Also of course since 2003 unmarried fathers do get automatic Parental Responsibility as long as they are on the birth certificate. This inconvenience can be avoided therefore by ensuring he is not on it; so the best plan is for you to attend the Registrar of Births without telling him.

Breast feeding is good for children and for you. The longer and more frequently you breast feed the harder it will be for your ex to see the baby for more than a few minutes at a time. Babies are very fragile and should only be fed by their primary carer, otherwise they can easily become ill.

Fathers are completely incapable of nurturing or loving their children, and of course, men can't cook, so always examine the contents of baby's nappy to see what father has fed him or indeed if he has fed him anything at all. In the hands of the father, something as innocuous as water can be dangerous to a baby even if it's straight out of the tap or a sealed bottle. There is no limit to a father's incompetence, and all the evidence to the contrary is plainly wrong.

Always fuss over your baby and cling on to them at handover. Insist on fastening any straps in a pushchair or child car seat yourself. Repeatedly kiss the baby and cry, saying 'Mummy loves you and is going to miss you so much' over and over until the child is crying too.

Never allow your baby to be taken out by their father if it is the least bit hot, cold, wet or windy, sunny, overcast, too dry or too humid.

If the weather is suitable for the baby to be taken out for a walk by his father make sure the baby is asleep the whole time, by keeping it awake for a few hours before he arrives. If the baby wakes and starts crying insist that it must be returned to you immediately for comforting, so ensure this is pointed out to any official and that the father is given strict instructions to comply with this. If he fails in this, you are, of course well within your rights to prevent the father seeing his child for a period of unspecified length, even when he promises to comply with your wishes.

Mothers automatically get parental responsibility. Fathers on the other hand, do not automatically get PR, unless they married you or they managed to get their name on the birth certificate. This is the clearest indication you could get that mothers are always responsible parents and fathers are merely wallets and sperm donors, and not to be trusted.

Chapter 3: All About Toddlers

Children are vulnerable and need to be protected from the world. The worst things that can happen to them is to have to grow up too soon and lose their childhood, or be saddled with a "loving" father. You have a duty to make sure they don't grow up too fast or get pushed into learning things they're not ready for, like sleeping in their own bed, weaning, potty training, etc. It's essential that they don't mature too quickly otherwise it might be argued that the father ought to be allowed to take them from you (something called contact) for whole nights at a time.

The mind of a toddler is like a sponge. They are very impressionable at this age, so it's essential you give them sound guidance and steer them in the right direction. Teach them to call your new partner Daddy and call your ex by his first name (or better still not call him at all).

The outside world is a dangerous place and it's important to explain to your toddler what's safe and normal and when they should stay near an adult they can trust. One technique is the "stranger danger" alert. The stranger the adult the greater the danger, so it's important to make sure that your ex becomes a complete stranger to his children. Then he can be really dangerous and you can get your children to be very frightened of him indeed. To protect your child you need to tell them their father is a really bad man who hit you and will hurt them and take them away from you, but if they stay with you they'll be safe..

Since toddlers are so vulnerable; mental, physical or sexual abuse and abduction are real threats, even though they may not ever have happened, and are likely never to happen. Try to ensure that your ex only has supervised contact at a contact centre.

It's important that your toddler feels secure and knows that you'll miss them and be thinking of them while they're away, so cry at handover and sob 'Mummy's going to miss you SO MUCH'. This lets them know you'll really miss them and they'll be welcomed back with open arms on their return. It also ensures they're thinking of you while they're away, because they will be worrying about you being upset.

If he does get more than a couple of hours contact send them in old/ragged/too small/unseasonable clothing with no spares.

If they come back in clothes that he has provided then:

1) Keep them

2) Reduce them to rags and send your child back in them

3) Send them back in the same clothes next time whatever the weather.

If they come back in clothes they are starting to grow out of, this is neglect. Take a photo and store this evidence up to use against him should the right opportunity arise.

Insist they should not be given fish fingers, even if it is the only thing they like. Instead send them with their own food so their diet is not disrupted.

Accuse him of giving them sweets. When you have made him stop, accuse him of not giving them treats.

If they bring a toy back from contact tell them it's dangerous, inappropriate or a weapon, and has to be disposed of immediately. Damage it yourself, and take a photo of it for future use in court.

Insist on inspecting his house before you allow the children to stay overnight there. Once you get it written into an order that you have to inspect the house, refrain from doing so as long as possible, in order to prevent the start of staying contact. Until you inspect the house no overnights can take place, so don't inspect it.

Chapter 4: All About School Aged Children

Non-Resident Parents and schools don't mix, it's a fact. Schools have enough on their plates so they don't want to deal with more than one parent for each child. In the interest of education it's your duty to make sure you don't confuse them by giving them more than one contact name and address and since you're the only parent which needs to know anything about the school, make sure to give them your details and not the father's.

If you use a childminder, make sure the school has their details too, because you approve of them, and they have care of the children, probably more than the ex. Even though they don't have PR , they're qualified to look after children, whereas the children's father has no experience and no such qualification.

Don't tell your ex anything about school, not even the school that you have applied for or which school the children have been accepted for. The longer you can keep this to yourself the better. Once they're at school, don't pass on anything from school that is meant for your ex.

Show the school every court order you get. Tell them your ex is dangerous and violent and should not be allowed in school, or even given any information regarding the children. If he is seen in the vicinity of the school you are to be notified at once as he's breaking the court order. Tell the school not to give the ex your address as you fear he might be dangerous. You will find that the school never asks for any evidence, so you can say you have court orders when you don't. Try it! It's so easy!

Despite keeping him in the dark, in the event that he turns up at a school concert or function immediately tell the Head his presence will upset the child and they will not be able to perform. Thanks to the universal prejudice against fathers, he will almost certainly be asked to leave and then you can enjoy the concert in peace, or, at the very least, enjoy his rage and frustration.

Tell the school your children have ADHD or are Autistic or have some other disorder that affects their behaviour and they need to have this investigated as it has been passed on from their father. There is no need to inform him of the referral to the schools special needs department because he's only the father. When he doesn't turn up for meetings it will prove that he is at fault, and might help the experts place the blame for bad behaviour at his door. If there is any event at school like sports day or a Christmas concert you think your ex may attend, keep the children at home and tell the school they are ill.

If the children say they want to spend more time with their father tell them the man ('Judge') said they couldn't spend more time. This will shift the blame from you to the court.

Chapter 5: Dealing With Teens

Teens are the difficult years. Every parent knows this but be reassured that when your teen is turning into a monosyllabic monster it's because they are taking after their father. It would be wise to remind them of this every time they do something you disapprove of. This works better on boys than girls. Boys generally then prefer to stay in their bedrooms and play with their computer where you can keep an eye on them. They won't have any troublesome friends and you can manage their social life effectively.

If they get depressed, refuse to go to college, smoke too much dope and remain unemployed, this is because they are like their father, and certainly not because having their father excluded from their lives has screwed them up. Living on benefits or off your ex is how you manage your life so it will be a good start for him. You can prove you love him by cooking, cleaning up, ironing, washing and generally mollycoddling him and he in return will show he can't live without you.

If he finds a girl friend he is bound to mistreat her and there is nothing you can do about it because he is just like his father and what do you expect?. If he gets too much to manage just remember that if he's out doors you can forget about him. As a sanction or punishment you can threaten to send him to his father. He will be frightened of this idea because of all the hours you have conscientiously put in, persuading him that his father is the root of all evil.

You must not pay attention to all this recent 'scientific research' about the value of having a proper relationship with both parents. Children may do much better in school, in life, in adult relationships; they may have greatly improved self-confidence, and be less likely to get into drugs, become pregnant or generally go off the rails. All this research must be a load of rubbish, otherwise the courts would make an effort to enforce their own orders for contact when you ignore or refuse to obey them.

Girls are a little easier to manage than boys. They look up to their mums and try to emulate them. If you treat them as your friend rather than your daughter they soon begin to share your values. They seem to understand instinctively that men are bad news but it's best if you remind them how much of a loser their Dad was whenever you can. This encourages them to avoid men, particularly as they haven't met any and don't understand them.

With luck she will learn there is no need for qualificatoins and when she discovers boys she may get pregnant quite quickly. She will believe like you that the father is a waster and you will be able to give her lots of advice about how to get rid of him and the bonus for you is that you will get another baby without all the aggravation of a relationship with a man. Girls tend to be easier because they are less likely to spend so much time in prison, as women, and particularly mothers, don't get sent to jail when a man would be.

Chapter 6: What's In A Name?

Your whole objective of course is to make your ex feel inferior or a second class parent, and there are many ways to achieve this such as:

- Changing your child's surname to yours. This is especially effective as it will infuriate him, especially if he is proud of his family tree.

- Getting your child to call their ex-parent by their first name.

- Getting your child to call your new partner "Daddy". This will have a profoundly negative effect on your ex and may even drive him into depression as he will feel totally ousted.

Another good trick is the use of derogatory nicknames for him. You want them to despise him so that they'll want to spend all the time with you. You might try, for example:

- 'That man'

- 'That useless waste of space'

- 'Kn*bhead/useless p**ck' etc - you get the idea and can think up your own.

The point is the children will soon pick up on it which is only to the good.

Chapter 7: Location, Location, Location

Moving away/abroad

A good way to get away from the ex is to move abroad. A court is very unlikely to stop you doing this even if the ex does get you to a court hearing before you manage to effect your move. It's especially unlikely you will be stopped if you are returning to your native country to be with family, are going to your new partner's native country to be with his family or are moving for work or to improve your lifestyle. The point is, the family courts pay scant or nil regard to the fact that your child is being ripped away from their home which they love, their school friends and family, their pets and their familiar surroundings. Make sure though that you use the notorious 'distress argument'; which simply explained means that if you are not allowed to have your way and go, you will be so distressed that you will be completely unable to nurture and bring up your child effectively; the judge will therefore always let you go. Let us assure you, it is a failsafe method to get what you want regardless of your children's wishes. Luckily, a father's distress counts for nothing at all, and may even be held as evidence of his instability.

Keeping your new address secret

You should always try to keep a new address secret. The ex might come round to your house and the children might catch sight of him outside designated contact times.

What to do if the ex-parent follows

If the ex parent moves to be near you when you have moved away just wait until he has settled into a new job and then move away again.

Handover Locations

The handover location should be your front door, or if you are keeping your address secret the front door of your parents or a friend. That way you can keep him waiting as long as you like.

Let the children see him but don't let them go to him which will be guaranteed to upset the children. Then you can claim they are so upset by the sight of their father there is no way you could force them to go with him.

Have all your family turn up to handovers. If something happens you've got plenty of witnesses to his behaviour, call the police and report him. Avoid having to go to a public place with CCTV for handover. It is too inconvenient. If you create a scene it will be caught on camera and provide him with proof that you started it and not him as you will allege.

Make sure he has them from Saturday morning to Sunday night on a weekend otherwise he might be able to pick them up from, and drop them off to school. This would spoil the impression of him that you've worked so hard to create with the teachers, and it won't allow you the chance to give the children the emotional support they need to get them through the ordeal by telling them how much you will miss them and how much you will cry and what fun activities they will be missing while away from you. Remember to cross examine them as soon as they leave him, in case anything happened that you can use against him.

Chapter 8: All About Grandparents

Paternal grandparents are unnecessary. Why would your children need more than two grandparents? That is enough for any kid. Your ex will be desperate for his parents to be involved with their grandchildren, as no doubt will they, and there is much talk nowadays about the benefit to the children of 'the wider family' but you really don't need to let all that 'pseudo research' worry you. You have a perfectly good family for them to be part of so why complicate matters?

In any case the paternal grandparents are old and not capable of looking after children. When they were younger they can't have been much good at it either, because just look at their offspring!

The paternal grandparents will interfere in the court process by making applications to see their grandchildren. This makes the whole process much longer and costlier, so it's better to erase the paternal family from your children's lives early. If being rude doesn't work; just tell the kids they needn't say thank you for the Xmas and birthday presents. Better still, don't pass the presents on and tell your children their father and his parents couldn't be bothered to buy them presents.

Tell everyone, certainly all the professionals, what a bad influence the paternal family have on the children. Dig out any barely related black sheep in their family and complain long and loud about them.

If you had a good relationship with any of the paternal family before you discovered what a rotter your ex was, use the connection to discredit your ex to his family. This often works surprisingly well.

Chapter 9: Special Occasions

On special occasions it's nice to be able to spend them with your family. It's not very nice to have to spend them with other people's families. Since your children only have one family now, it's in their interest to spend all those special occasions with you.

Christmas is one of the most special occasions of the year. The problem is that Christmas is so expensive. If both of you buy your presents before Christmas, you'll both be paying full price. After Christmas the sales are on and the prices drop. This is particularly true of all the special Christmas paraphernalia, which only gets sold at that time of year.

Do try to ensure that your children don't get the presents and cards that he sends, and if he telephones to speak to them, you can easily think of excuses to fob him off. Then tell the children that he has forgotten about them and obviously doesn't love them anymore. Promise to ring him back, and then don't.

Since children will be with their proper family at Christmas, best thing is for the ex not to see them until after the sales have started. That way Christmas will be cheaper for them and they'll find it easier to buy presents and afford all the maintenance they have to pay you. Tell them they can see the children on or after 28th December. If you've got a New Years Eve party to go to you could delay this until the 31st, that way you can claim you're sharing the holidays equally, the children have Christmas with you and New Year with that other person.

The Courts may suggest that the children spend alternative Christmas with you and your ex; but you know that it is much more important that they are with you for this family occassion. You won't find it too hard to arrange things so that the children always spend Christmas with you. He is very likely to give in to 'keep the peace'; as long as you allow him a visit at some stage at your convenience.

Chapter 10: Using Technology for Communication

You don't want to talk to the ex, why would you? He's always asking for some favour, usually more time with the kids, which he cannot be allowed under any circumstances. The court order gives the maximum contact time and you should always try to get away with even less. When the children are with your ex you need to speak to them frequently, which prevents them relaxing into their time with their father, but he should never be allowed to speak to them when they are with you.

When communicating with the ex

- *Don't answer the phone to him, he may catch you unawares and get your agreement to something. This will cause him to text or email more frequently. Keep records because this can be called harassment.*

- *Send him texts accusing him or complaining about him, which you can use as evidence that he must have been harassing you.*

- *Always text him when you know it will be inconvenient. e.g. when he is driving*

- *Never answer his questions; preferably, hit him with a tirade of abuse.*

- *Save all his texts to present to court as evidence of his harassment of you and abuse of your children. Phone him at work and if he is unavailable ask to speak to his boss. Keep his boss on the phone as long as possible complaining about his violence and lack of child maintenance.*

When communicating with your children

- *Always insist on your children communicating with you at least once a day while they are with the ex.*

- *Specify times that you know will be inconvenient and/or will be a tricky moment emotionally. E.g. thirty minutes after a tearful handover because you know they won't have settled yet. At bedtime ring to tell your children how much you love and miss them, and how you have cried since they left.*

- *Give them a phone to call you on and insist they carry it all the time so you can call them whenever you feel like it.*

- *Tell them about all the wonderful things they are missing at your home.*

When your ex wants to communicate with your children

- *Claim any phone they bring home is lost or broken.*

- *Claim your phone has a flat battery*

- *Claim you don't have the internet*

- *Claim you don't know how to set up Skype*

If he does manage to talk to any of your children

- *Tell them loudly to hang up straight away*
- *Grab the phone, swear at him and hang up*
- *Claim it is mealtime and they can't talk.*
- *Whisper to them what to say*

If it is Skype

- *Stand behind the screen and gesture to the children to finish the conversation*
- *Whisper or mouth to them what to say*
- *Shout abuse at him*
- *Pull the plug/shutdown the computer*
- *Stand behind your child making V signs and mouthing 'W****R'*

Chapter 11: All About Doctors, Dentists & Healthcare Professionals

Tell your doctor how violent your ex has been and how ill it makes you, and ask him to write a letter to the court setting out everything you have told him as if he has witnessed it himself.

Take your children to the local Children's Centre claiming they have behaviour problems due to their father having ADHD/Autism/OCD/BPD and ask for the children to be assessed.

When asked if the father can be contacted and involved in assessment refuse permission for him to be told anything. Say you don't know where he lives.

Tell everyone your ex is violent and dangerous and they should not be alone with him. This will cause all professionals to try to avoid him; but if they have to see him, to ensure there are at least two of them present.

As you may already know Doctors are very supportive and keen listeners. Just as you can get them to give you a doctor's certificate if you fancy a few days off work, you can also get them to write letters "To whom it may concern" detailing the stress and anguish the ex is putting you under. A lot of them are willing to repeat in writing anything you tell them, completely free of charge. After all they have no reason to think what you're saying isn't true, why would you lie?

Ensure all healthcare professionals are told thatthere's a court order in place banning your ex from having contact with the kids, except at specific times. They won't check and will refuse to talk to him.

Chapter 12: Supporting Your Child

How to Maximise Your Parent Maintenance Payments.

Child Maintenance, or to give it its proper title, Sole Parent Support, is a form of taxation invented by the Government to punish you child's ex-parent, and serves them right too. You can tell it's punishment taxation because it bears no relation to the actual cost of raising a child, it's simply there to deprive the ex-parent of any spare cash they might otherwise have used to entice your child away from loving you alone.

Since getting rid of the unwanted other parent is so stressful for you, the kind people in Westminster have decided that you need extra money for pastimes and hobbies such as shopping and getting your hair done. After all you want to look your best for your child and have all the latest toys and games so they'll want what's best for themselves, namely to stay with you.

This loyalty scheme rewards you for removing that distracting ex-parent from your poor darling's life by giving you more money the less time your confused little baby has to spend with that monster. Let's face it, the ex never spends any money on your child anyway, because you've heisted it, nor do they have the lovely house you have, so full of toys, because you've heisted that too. They can't even be bothered to get a place with a bedroom for your darlings, saying that they can't afford it, so they're bound to waste all that money anyway. You can put it to much better use.

You can see from the so called 'Bedroom Tax' that the government doesn't think it's a good idea for your ex to have a spare room to make a bedroom for your child, therefore overnights MUST be a bad thing.

Chapter 13: All About Property and Finance

Property

After you separate from the NRP you'll need to sort out the property and the money, and make sure that you get it even if you never contributed anything at all. The golden rule here is that possession is 9/10ths of the law. The most important thing is to get sole possession of the family home. The best way to do this is with an Occupation Order, combined with a Non Molestation Order. You'll need the latter because the NRP is undoubtedly going to be furious when evicted from his own home, so your life will probably be in danger.

If you have already left your home because he was so unbearable (see the section on Domestic Abuse) then don't worry, not all is lost. You can still get all your precious possessions back without him interfering. The best way is to lull him into a false sense of security by making an agreement in principle to divide the assets fairly between the two of you.

This is important as you know he has a bit of a temper and can fly off the handle at a moments notice. The process of separation is stressful enough so it's important not to upset him too much at present, so make sure he's fully aware of the arrangements. Once you've calmed him down arrange a date some time in the future when both of you can oversee the collection of your share. In order to arrange this you'll need to get his schedule to know when he's going to be at home.

The process of collecting your belongings can be extremely emotional for the NRP, so you owe it to him to do this in the least traumatic way possible. He may think that he needs to be there, but it's much better if he isn't, so, having found out when he won't be there, go to the house when he's away and collect your things then, and as many of his things as you fancy.

You may have had some disagreement about what you should have and what he should keep. This is the time to correct his misunderstanding and reclaim what's rightfully yours. Don't worry about leaving him without what you might consider bare essentials, like a 3 piece suite, dining table, television or bed, NRP's don't get much chance to relax, eat or sleep, so he won't be needing those things anymore.

Make sure you remove any personal items which might remind him of your life together. It's particularly important to remove any photos or memorabilia which might remind him of your children. Moping over your children will affect his work and now you've got a new home to maintain he needs to work all the hours available to keep you in the style to which you're accustomed.

Finances

The first thing to do is to prevent him spending any of your money that's in joint accounts or running up a huge credit card bill at your expense. You can go to the bank or building society and ask them to freeze the account, but this is a bit of an administrative nightmare and only leads to more money wasted on solicitors when you come to sort out the finances. The simplest way to reduce the complexity of sorting out the finances is to empty the joint accounts into your own private account. Once there the money belongs to you and you can use it for those little essentials which he doesn't understand.

Similarly with the credit cards:- to protect yourself you need to make sure he can't run up a debt at your expense by spending on them, so you need to max them out yourself. It may seem a bit too noble taking on all this burden on your own, but don't worry the court will make sure you each get a fair share of the debt so he won't lose out.

Chapter 14: All About Making Allegations

If you have to have a psychological assessment, spend the time crying and telling the psychologist how dreadful your ex is and how ill it makes you. This will result in him running out of time to do the standard tests and therefore he will not be able to write up a full report on you.

Think up all the nasty things you can say about him. Tell everyone all of it. Several times. Add more as you think of it. Tell Cafcass, social workers , police, psychologists, doctors, the nursery, the school, the childminder, your friends and family. Before long you will believe it all and be able to tell the story with absolute conviction. When you get to court they are bound to believe you.

If you make allegations of domestic violence to women's organisations they will whisk you and the children off to a refuge. The best thing about a refuge is that you will meet many other mothers who have had lots of experiences and you can learn from them.   The ex won't know where you are and nobody will tell him. Peace and quiet at last. Your will get a sympathetic social worker who will help you with CSA payments, housing benefits and other income. Then you will be given local authority accommodation with a bedroom for each of your kids. You might even get Xmas hampers and toys for the kids from local charities

If you feel so inclined, tell the police he sexually abused the children. He will be arrested and by the time he has cleared his name you and the children can be long gone. With a bit of luck he will never find you again. Don't worry about lying; the family courts are renowned for doing absolutely nothing about this, and perjury is so prevalent that it is practically expected of you.

If you feel you need extra support with all this try Netmums:

http://www.netmums.com/home/netmums-campaigns/get-families-talking-about-separating

Chapter 15: All About Family Courts

In the unlikely event that you haven't been able to get rid of that annoying parent and the ex is foolish enough to make an application to the Family Courts this chapter contains all the advice you'll need to turn this to your advantage.

Domestic Violence

Firstly you need to understand and accept that you are a victim of domestic violence. You may not realise it, your ex may never have retaliated when you hit him, but they were violent none the less. Just remember that simply making an application to court is an act of aggression by your ex and demonstrates that they can't co-operate and they are hell bent on persecuting you by using your child as a weapon and dragging you through the Family Courts.

Domestic Violence takes many forms:

- *Psychological*
  - *Controlling behaviour*
  - *Mind Games*
  - *Using "Logic" when arguing his case*
  - *Not replying to your text messages immediately*
  - *Not letting you have the last word*
  - *Being interested in football*
  - *Not doing what you want immediately*
- *Physical*
  - *Physical contact of any kind, e.g. brushing up against you*
  - *Hurting your hand when you slapped or punched him*
  - *Grabbing your wrists when you pummel his chest*
- *Sexual*
  - *Forcing you to have sex with him against your will*
  - *Deciding after the event that it was against your will*
  - *Not being available for sex when you want*
  - *Not accepting that you have sexual needs that need satisfying elsewhere*
- *Financial*
  - *Not giving you a credit card or not paying off your credit card when you hit the limit.*

- *Not giving you cash when you've run out*

- *Telling you to use your income to pay household bills instead of buying what you want*

- *Trying to limit your shoe collection*

- *Emotional*

  - *Telling you to lose/gain weight*

  - *Not apologising for upsetting you*

  - *Claiming not to realise he is upsetting you*

  - *Not being able to mind-read*

  - *Making a noise when he eats Corn Flakes*

If you think carefully it should be possible for you to think of cases where your ex had perpetrated every type of Domestic Violence listed above against you. Don't worry if the ex has never been cruel or abusive to your child, it's what they did to you that matters in the Family Courts, despite the fact that you will have gone there over your children's contact issues .

Examples of serious psychological Domestic Violence are:

- *Having rules about mixing colours in the washing machine or how the dishwasher is loaded.*

- *Your ex complaining they can't find things after you've cleaned up and tidied away.*

- *He gives you the silent treatment or cold shoulder.*

- *He bullied you by being taller/larger/stronger than you.*

- *He doesn't like Strictly Come Dancing.*

If you need help documenting your allegations of Domestic Violence, there are several organisations who can help. Women's Aid have a very useful manual on identifying Domestic Violence you have been subjected to. If you really can't remember any of the things he's done, it's probably PTSD, your memory has been affected by his violence, or it will upset you too much to bring it all up again. If he hasn't yet committed DV against you, it's important to tell the court you are in fear of him because he may commit DV against you.

That you are 'afraid' of him or that he is 'intimidating' you, or is 'bullying' you, are three great expressions that you can use again and again in court and will unfailingly have a beneficial effect. Demanding to see his children is 'bullying', and weeping down the phone or begging at your door is too.

Criminalising the ex

As has been mentioned before, you are a victim. You may not be able to secure a conviction for the Domestic Violence you suffered, but you can get him convicted of other crimes.

Harassment

If the ex tries to contact you in any way, whether it's about your children or any other matter, this is harassment. Unfortunately the police won't arrest him immediately, but you can get them to issue a Police Information Notice (PIN). This is a piece of paper telling your ex what he did wrong and warning him that if he does it again, ever, then he will be arrested. What was it he did again? Oh it doesn't matter, we all know that fathers are feckless and irrelevant, and given that the police are issuing PINs left right and centre to these fathers, they must all be bad-uns so best to get one issued as soon as possible.

Solicitors

Solicitors can be very expensive, however see the previous section on Domestic Violence to find out what form of DV you have suffered during the relationship or since separation. In this case you are eligible for Legal Aid. In order to prove you are a victim you will need to provide one of the following forms of evidence (taken from:

http://www.justice.gov.uk/legal-aid-for-private-family-matters/legal-aid-divorcing-separating-abusive-partner):

Types of evidence which are accepted:

- *Criminal conviction*

- *Police caution*

- *Ongoing criminal proceedings*

- *Protective injunction*

- *An undertaking*

- *Letter from a Multi Agency Risk Assessment Conference*

- *Finding of fact, by a court*

- *Letter from social services*

- *Letter from a GP, doctor, nurse, midwife or healthcare professional*

- *Letter from a domestic violence refuge*

It may be difficult to get a criminal conviction or criminal proceedings against your ex, as these require proof beyond reasonable doubt, but the last 3 forms of evidence of Domestic Violence are quite easy to obtain without any proof. GPs are a pushover; it's as easy as getting a sick note. Social services are generally staffed by single parent mothers, just like you, and they will be most sympathetic. Remember Domestic Violence can take many forms and most of them leave no physical or psychological trace, so you can avoid having to prove anything or coming up with any facts.

The simplest way to get evidence of domestic violence is to stay at a refuge for victims of domestic violence for 24 hours and ask them to fill in a letter to evidence this. It is not necessary to have any physical injuries and you will not be examined or assessed in any meaningful way. If the refuge doesn't already have a form for this, let them know the government provides templates at http://www.justice.gov.uk/legal-aid-for-private-family-matters. The refuge staff will have done it many times.

Once armed with a free solicitor you are much better able to prevent the ex succeeding in their application. If you have told everyone how violent he is and how afraid you are you will get Legal Aid and the state will pay for your solicitor and barrister. The solicitors will extend and complicate matters nicely so your ex will see no or very little progress, and completely run out of money because of his legal bills. Meanwhile you can claim child support. Eventually he will give up just as he did with the decorating and the garden.

Your solicitor should delay everything as much as possible so that it is an eternity until the ex gets any contact. When you make a position statement put in all your grievances; include everything from the year dot. The judge will want to know how awful your ex is. You can even argue that it's been so long since the kids saw their father that contact should be no more that 1 hour a month so they can get used to him again slowly.

Solicitors like sport, particularly Tennis. However they don't play traditional tennis, they play letter tennis. This is a slow, expensive and drawn out game where the aim is to transfer the assets of their clients to their own bank accounts by means of useless pieces of paper, called solicitor's letters, bounced between themselves. The game ends when one or other of the clients gives up or runs out of money.

Further tips and tricks

- *Refuse mediation and get him to take you to court. If you have legal aid because of accusing him of DV, this will ensure that his legal representation costs him a fortune while yours is free.*

- *Lose any paperwork you are given*

- *Cancel contact at the last minute due to illness*

- *Expect your ex to baby-sit at very short notice (if he can't, deny contact next time)*

- *Ask for extra money for children's presents*

- *If you only have short term leave to remain in the UK accuse him of DV. Then you can apply for a full British passport and will usually get one.*

- *Once you have your passport apply for Council Housing*

- *If you ex is still living in your shared Council House withdraw your name from the lease and he will become homeless allowing you to re-apply or take over his home.*

- *Never put any of the above in writing*

Court Hearings

If you have a solicitor, the best thing to do is avoid going to hearings altogether unless you are ordered to attend. Tell your solicitor to say you have been unable to arrange alternative childcare or that the stress of the court proceedings is too much for you.

If you do have to attend court, make sure you ask for an escort and enter the courtroom by a different entrance to your ex because you've suffered domestic abuse. If you have an ounce of principle you can say you are afraid he might commit domestic violence. When you go to court always dress demurely, wear little or no make up, look terrified and look at the floor. Answer questions in a whisper and keep saying 'sorry'. This way a male judge will inevitably feel sorry for you and automatically be on your side. This does not work so well with female judges.

If your ex is allowed to cross examine you in court always cry and answer each question very quietly so the Judge can't hear.

Court Orders

There are several types of court order which a court can make when an application is brought before the court. They are in order of importance:

a) Non-Molestation Orders

   i) Every single parent should have one of these, otherwise the ex WILL harass and molest you.

   ii) They're also useful for schools so the police can be called if he's seen in the vicinity, trying to abduct the children.

b) Child Arrangement Orders

   i) So the ex knows the children live with you and only 'spend time with' him

   ii) So everyone can see you're the good, responsible parent: that's why the court decided they should live with you.

c) Prohibited Steps Orders

   i) Telling the ex all the things he mustn't do

d) Specific Issue Orders

   i) These are where the court tells your ex you were right all along.

e) There used to be one more - Contact Orders

   i) These have now been discontinued by the Children and Families Act 2014 which decided you only ever need to know who the child lives with and sometimes you can thrown the ex a bone by allowing him to see your children.

The Children & Families Act 2014 which came into force on 22nd April 2014 replaced Residence and Contact Orders with a new single Child Arrangements Order. This may seem a little confusing at first, but don't worry, the Family Law Industry has sorted this out. It's now clear that it's just a renaming of familiar roles.

With the advent of the Children Act 1989, Contact and Residence replaced the terms Custody and Access, but basically came to mean the same thing. The Family Law Industry has ensured that a form of words is chosen when making Child

Arrangement Order which has exactly the same meaning as Custody and Access, so even though everything changes it all remains exactly the same.

Children's Wishes and Feelings

Naturally, as much you wish that ex to disappear, so do your children. After all, they are your children and it's only natural that they think and feel like you. If, for some reason, difficult to imagine here, the Domestic Violence clause does not bring you much deserved relief, you should turn your attention to another highly efficient tool, that of the children's wishes. If you observe carefully, and use your imagination productively, you will realise that your children hate the ex with the same passion that you do. It is obvious, how could your children feel otherwise? You should carefully note that 'The Children's Wishes' is a rather longer term plan and may take slightly longer to accomplish, but if you persevere the results are as good as assured. The trick is to keep them away from their father until they only have a hazy memory of him and their affection for him has been eroded.

When you invoke the Children's Wishes con you will have already been made aware of this by your counsel. If not he/she failed you, so dismiss and change your counsel. They should tell you the judge will likely order a Wishes & Feeling report on your children. It will depend somewhat on the age of your children but in some cases such reports were ordered on children as young as 7-8 where they were asked why they don't want to see their ex-parent. You need of course to work on them systematically, as you always do, so that when these reports are ordered your children already have a clear view of what they want, why they want it and the way to express it. It should not be too difficult for you. All you need is to talk with your children as any good parent would, and explain to them what they want, why this is good and what's the best way to express it to an already sympathetic Cafcass officer. A word of warning here: Some judges are getting quite good at working out that the child's wishes are in fact your wishes and say annoying things like: 'he/she seems to me to be talking in age inappropriate language. So do bear this in mind and ensure they give your (sorry- their) wishes in language appropriate to their age. This way you will fool both the Cafcass Officer and the Judge. There have been occasions in the past where loving mothers, wishing to spare their children the anguish of constant hope, have declared the ex-father to have died. When the children find out many years later that in fact their father is alive and well, this could possibly rebound on you; but by then they will be adults so you shouldn't worry too much about that.

If done carefully, persistently, the process of Children's Wishesand Feelings can be dragged on for years, in and out of courts and contact centres, and yields excellent results. 'But that will cost me a fortune' I hear you cry! Not if you have accused him of DV to get Legal Aid it won't. But of course it will cost him a fortune and he may well be forced to give up, so it becomes a win/win situation for you! Bear in mind that if you force him to run out of money because of legal fees, then you won't be able to claim it off him for yourself, however.

Make sure you have a dictaphone or other recording device handy and record every bad thing the children say about the ex, particularly when you tell them they have to go and see him and they refuse. This always convinces courts of the sincerity of their feelings and that you are totally justified in stopping contact with the other parent. Such recordings do take a certain amount of rehearsal time, but the effort is worth it.

Glossary of Terms

Applicant   In the case of a Non Resident Parent (NRP) making the application this is the bully who is persecuting you by taking you to court. If it's you who made the application, it's the protector of your children

Cafcass   Children and Family Court Advisory and Support Service (court social workers). They advise judges.

CAO   Child Arrangement Orders are a new name for the old Contact and Residence orders, but will basically have the same effect.

DV/DA   Domestic Violence, anything he has said/done that you don't like or anything you can make up he's said/done that will serve the same purpose - to get him branded a bad person and win legal aid for yourself.

Ex   ex- (or soon to be ex-) parent or partner

NRP   Newly Redundant Parent, the one who left you because he's worthless and no good, or that you kicked out for any old reason that occurred to you at the time.

OO   Occupation Order - an order which gives you the sole right to the house and keeps him at least 100 yards away. Very useful in that if he steps over the line you can have him arrested.

NMO   Non Molestation Order. - Useful in that it stops him coming near you or communicating with you

PR   Parental Responsibility - An unimportant legal technicality which can be circumvented by the appropriate use of mis-information on your part.

PWC   Parent With Care - The Mother obviously, except for the 10% of cases where the courts discriminate against mothers.

RO   Residence Order - must be in your favour, obviously, as the children live with you.

Respondent see Applicant and reverse the roles.

RP   Resident Parent - the primary and only important parent.

SIO   Specific issue order - to stop him doing something specific like giving the children a hair cut, or taking them to the dentist.

SRO   Shared Residence Order - to be avoided at all costs as it signals to the world that the children have two equal parents and causes the children to have to put up with all that 'having two homes' nonsense that they actually rather like. This type of order is as rare as hen's teeth. Fortunately abolished by the Children and Families Act 2014.

Disclaimer

These techniques are dangerous so do not use them without the guidance of a trained professional. For legal reasons it must be pointed out that wherever we use he, him or his you could also use she, her or hers and vice-versa, except where we refer to biological matters which only relate to one sex. You might think this means that parenting and the Family Courts are non-gender specific, but rest assured that although there is no significant gender bias in the legislation, on the balance of probability 9 times out of 10 residency and all the benefits which that accords will be granted to the mother irrespective of her parenting ability, and even if she is a junkie or an alcoholic.

It should be noted that all 'tricks & tips' listed in this volume have been extensively tested and proved effective. Rigorous research is backed by real life experience and tested out either on the authors or on their friends and family. Some are more popular than others.

Also by the same authors

Childcare for Single Parents: How to keep the benefits of having children without the nuisance of actually caring for them.

Now you've managed to get rid of that annoying other parent, you'll need a way to keep the children out from under your feet. Suggestions on after school clubs, holiday clubs and various electronic babysitting devices such as television, DVDs and video games which will replace that exhausting physical exercise, outings and boring paternal family which made your children so unhappy to come back to you.

Keeping Children Clean & Safe

How to keep your kids clean and avoid football, parks, gardens, cycling, camping, climbing trees, DIY and other mess and dirt related activities. A must for the busy single parent.

DIY for the Single Parent

A host of psychological techniques for extracting DIY efforts from men without the complications of money, emotional involvement or mess.

Printed in Great Britain
by Amazon

60730060R00020